371.30281

...ning
and
note-taking

Nicolas Ferguson
Máire O'Reilly

CELL
centre for the experimentation
and evaluation
of language learning techniques

Evans

Published by Evans Brothers Limited
Montague House, Russell Square,
London WC1B 5BX

Evans Brothers (Nigeria Publishers) Limited
PMB 5146, Jericho Road
Ibadan

First published by CEEL 1977
First published by Evans Brothers Limited 1978

Acknowledgements

We are grateful for permission to reproduce copyright material
to the World Health Organisation, Geneva for Talks 1, 3, 4, 7,
9, 16, 22, 32, 33, 34, 36, 37, 42, 44, 46, 48, and for the
photographs on pages 8, 16, 20, 28, 32, 36, 40, 44 and 77;
to the University of Chicago Press for Text 2 from *Managerial
Psychology* by H. J. Leavitt, 1972; and to *Punch* for the cartoons
on pages 12, 54, 55 and 75.

Cover illustration by Josef Stojan

W13284 £1.55. 8.80

Filmset and printed by
BAS Printers Limited, Over Wallop, Hampshire

ISBN 0 237 50224 0   PRA 6100

Contents

Introduction

This book has been written for all those who need to listen to talks and retain a large proportion of what is said. This will include students, and those who attend meetings, conferences, lectures . . .

It is directed towards both native speakers of English and intermediate and advanced students of English as a foreign language.

This course has been made partially for self-instruction. Many of the talks, however, touch on controversial topics. Since discussion can help deepen an understanding of what has been heard and stimulate further listening, the most effective way of using this course is in a group where such discussion is possible.

Listening is a skill that is by no means limited to attending lectures. When we are in the living-room, we may be listening for a noise in the kitchen which suggests that dinner is ready; we may be listening to someone giving a vivid description of an accident; we may be listening to someone with half an ear while reading the newspaper at the same time . . . The following are the main types of listening.

Casual Listening
Conversational listening: listening in social interaction.
Secondary listening: listening to background sounds to make other primary activity more meaningful.
Aesthetic listening: listening for the enjoyment of content with no thought of discussing critically.

Creative Listening
Reconstructing the image and feelings suggested by what one is hearing.

Exploratory Listening
Random listening to find points of interest.

Intent Listening
Receptive listening:
remembering a sequence of details

Reflective listening: getting central ideas
identifying transitional elements
using contextual clues to determine word meaning
distinguishing relevant and irrelevant material
drawing inferences

This course trains the last category: intent listening.

A Method of Study

Above all, this book presents a method of study that can subsequently be used to train and practise listening comprehension with other recorded talks.

The Difficulty of the Extracts

All but the shortest talks have been rated for difficulty on a seven-point scale as follows:

Difficulty	Style	Example
1	very easy	comic
2	easy	
3	fairly easy	popular
4	standard	
5	fairly difficult	quality
6	difficulty	academic
7	very difficult	scientific

As this book has been designed for intermediate to advanced level students of English, the majority of the passages used are in the difficulty range 4–7.

Part 1   Immediate recall exercises

The way these exercises are studied will depend on whether a
language laboratory is available or not.

If a language laboratory is available

1   Each text has been recorded twice: once without interruption and
once with questions. Each text is divided into small sections of 20–40
words, and after each section there are two or three questions.
For example:

Deaths by drowning are common everywhere. In the United States
alone, about 7,000 children under four drown each year.
    3   What accidents are common everywhere?
    4   What country is mentioned?
    5   What's the accident rate in this country from drowning?

First listen to the unbroken version. Then listen to the version with
questions and try to answer these orally in the spaces provided on
the tape.

If you can't answer a question, rewind your tape and listen to the
relevant information before trying again.

2   When you have answered all the questions, rewind to the beginning
of the tape, and shadow the uninterrupted version three seconds
behind the speaker.

To shadow the exercise, listen to the recording. As soon as the
speaker starts, count 'one thousand and one, one thousand and two,
one thousand and three,' and then start repeating the same text just
behind the voice on the tape. Whenever you have a problem, stop
your recorder and practise the sentence in question. You must then
return to the beginning of the tape and start again. At each
subsequent difficulty, you should stop, practise, and then start the
exercise again *from the beginning.*

Such an exercise demands full participation and, if carried out
successfully, is very rewarding. It is especially useful in training
fluency and in pointing out where your problems lie since, as soon as
you have any difficulty, no matter how slight, you block.

3   In this book there is a brief outline of each text. Using the outline as

a guide, rewrite the text in your own words. Then turn to the transcript of the text and correct what you have done.

4 Working with a second person, narrate the text using the outline to guide you, while the other person, using the transcript, corrects you.

If a language laboratory is not available

The best way is to work in a small group under the guidance of a teacher. The group is split into sub-groups of two or three.

1 The whole text is heard without interruption.

2 The first part of the broken up version is heard, together with the first set of questions.

Students answer in writing.

The section is played again, and the questions are played a second time. Within each group, students debate the answers. The teacher will answer questions that are asked concerning meaning.

The section will be replayed until everyone is satisfied he has an answer to each question.

The answers are given out loud, and any points of disagreement discussed.

This procedure continues for each segment.

3 In this book there is a brief outline of each text. Using the outline as a guide, rewrite the text in your own words. Then turn to the transcript of the text and correct what you have done.

4 Working with a second person, narrate the text using the outline to guide you, while the other person, using the transcript, corrects you.

1 The Water Babies

Outline

Drowning   Man does not swim instinctively
               Deaths by drowning are common
               In the USA, 7,000 children drown yearly

Classes   Babies are taught to swim
               Aged from 7 to 24 months
               Classes in Florida and California
               Several European countries run courses

Learning   Babies learn quickly
process   Eradicate fear
               Floating
               Breathing
               Arm and leg movements
               Swims by himself

✦ *Transcript

All mammals, except man and the monkey, swim naturally from birth. For man, like the monkey, it is not instinctive to float. Deaths by drowning are common everywhere. In the United States alone, about 7,000 children under four drown each year.

Everything possible's done to prevent such tragedies. One solution's particularly effective – teaching children to swim while they are still babies. Most large towns in Florida and California already run lessons for babies and infants. The idea has spread to Europe where, in several countries, special courses are now arranged for children from seven to twenty-four months.

The first step's to eradicate the child's fear of the water. Next, he's taught to float. Once he can do this naturally and without fear, the child grasps the technique and can propel himself through the water.

135 words; Difficulty 2

* This article was first published in 1972. The statistics are for that year.

Immediate recall

All mammals, except man and the monkey, swim naturally from birth. For man, like the monkey, it is not instinctive to float.
1　What animals swim from birth?
2　What's not instinctive for man?

Deaths by drowning are common everywhere. In the United States alone, about 7,000 children under four drown each year.
3　What accidents are common everywhere?
4　Which country is mentioned?
5　What's the accident rate in this country from drowning?

Everything possible's done to prevent such tragedies. One solution is particularly effective – teaching children to swim while they are still babies.
6　What's done to prevent these accidents?
7　What solution's effective?

Most large towns in Florida and California already run lessons for babies and infants. The idea has spread to Europe where, in several countries, special courses are now arranged for children from seven to twenty-four months.
8　Where are courses run?
9　Where's the idea spread to?
10　Between what ages are courses arranged?

The first step's to eradicate the child's fear of the water. Next, he's taught to float.

11 What's the first step?

12 What's the second step?

Once he can do this naturally and without fear, the teacher can move on to breathing, and arm and leg movements. Before long, the child grasps the technique and can propel himself through the water.

13 What's the third step?

14 What does the child grasp before long?

15 What does he learn to do?

Further discussion

1 What other accidents could we avoid by training babies and small children?

2 How could this training be carried out?

'I think it's cruel the way they keep them cooped up in those little cages.'

Outline

Differences	Different people see things differently
Cause	Relevance to needs affects our perception
	Aids are seen quickly
	Non-dangerous obstacles are seen and then denied
	Dangerous obstacles are perceived
Our act	We try to give a good impression
	We act
	Success depends on picking up audience reactions
	Audience reactions are difficult to pick up
	The audience is acting too
Remedy	We must not ignore differences in perception
	It is easy to suppose everyone perceives the same way
	Time spent in reaching a common view is well invested

Transcript

People see things differently. Even 'facts' may be seen quite differently by different people. Relevance to one's needs is the most important determinant of one's personal view of the world. Things that seem to be aids to satisfying one's needs are seen quickly. But things that look like obstacles, if they are not critically threatening, may also be seen quickly, only then to be denied so that they appear not to have been seen at all. By denying obstacles, people 'protect' themselves temporarily from them. If they really become dangerous, however, people drop the blinkers and face the obstacles.

One of the things we perceive is ourselves and other people. To protect and enhance ourselves, we try to manipulate the picture other people have of us by putting up a front that will make them think we are what we want to be. The problem of our act, and getting it across successfully, depends mostly on our ability to pick up audience reactions accurately. And accurate audience reactions are hard to come by because the audience is acting too.

To ignore differences in perception is to ignore a major determinant of behaviour. Yet it is easy to assume unjustifiably that everyone views the world from the same perspective as the viewer. Time spent trying to reach a common view is not wasted time.

223 words; Difficulty 4

Immediate recall

People see things differently. Even 'facts' may be seen quite differently by different people. Relevance to one's needs is the most important determinant of one's personal view of the world.

1 How are people said to see things?
2 What's mentioned about 'facts'?
3 What consideration most determines one's view of the world?

Things that seem to be aids to satisfying one's needs are seen quickly. But things that look like obstacles, if they are not critically threatening, may also be seen quickly, only then to be denied so that they appear not to have been seen at all.

4 What sorts of things are seen quickly?
5 What other sorts of things are seen quickly, but then denied?
6 Once denied, how do these obstacles appear?
7 What's the condition for ignoring obstacles?

By denying obstacles, people 'protect' themselves temporarily from them. If they really become dangerous, however, people drop the blinkers and face the obstacles.

8 What do people do by denying obstacles?

9 If obstacles really become dangerous, what do people do?

One of the things we perceive is ourselves and other people. To protect and enhance ourselves, we try to manipulate the picture other people have of us by putting up a front that will make them think we are what we want to be.

10 What are we said to perceive?
11 What do we do to protect and enhance ourselves?

The problem of our act, and getting it across successfully, depends mostly on our ability to pick up audience reactions accurately. And accurate audience reactions are hard to come by, because the audience is acting too.

12 What ability does the success of our act depend on?
13 Why are audience reactions hard to interpret accurately?

To ignore differences in perception is to ignore a major determinant of behaviour. Yet it is easy to unjustifiably assume that everyone views the world from the same perspective as the viewer. Time spent trying to reach a common view is not wasted time.

14 Name a major determinant of behaviour.
15 What's easy for an individual viewer to assume?
16 What's it worth spending time to reach?

Further discussion

1 A husband asks his wife what she did all day. He wants to sound interested. The wife immediately starts crying because she thinks he is trying to point out that she never does anything.

Can you think of any other examples of differences in perception?

2 In what ways do people try and manipulate the picture others have of them?

3 It has been said that the most successful people are simply the most successful actors. What do you think?

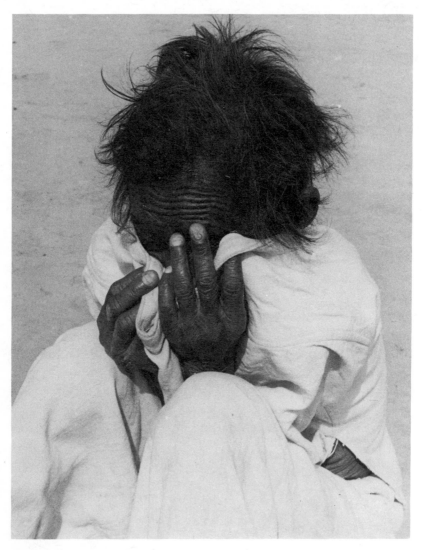

Mind and body are integrated.

Outline

Definition Mind and Body are integrated
      Abandoned children lose hair
      A boy with a falsetto voice can keep a cold
      The study is called psychosomatics

Diagnosis Different personality types get different diseases
      Stress can cause disease
      Investigators are collecting evidence
      Personality can help diagnosis

Children seem to lose hair as a response to feeling abandoned. A young man whose squeaky voice was a standing joke to his friends unconsciously clung to a cold for weeks at a time because it made him sound husky. These are examples of a field of investigation called psychosomatics, in which the mind and body are considered integrated parts of the whole being, and both aspects are examined together.

Studies have shown that a continuing state of emotional stress can cause physical changes that lead to disease. The most provocative conclusion that has so far been produced, however, is that different personality types tend to get different diseases.

Some investigators are amassing impressive evidence to show that there's a significant link between the kind of person you are and the kind of bodily disease you're prone to. The results of a study by the psychiatrist Dr Floyd O. Ring would appear to support the conclusion that 'People with some illnesses can be picked out with a good percentage of accuracy by personality alone.'

175 words; Difficulty 5

Immediate recall

Children seem to lose hair as a response to feeling abandoned. A young man whose squeaky voice was a standing joke to his friends unconsciously clung to a cold for weeks at a time because it made him sound husky.
1   What's one cause of children's losing hair?
2   Why did the young man in the example cling to a cold?

These are examples of a field of investigation called psychosomatics, in which the mind and body are considered integrated parts of the whole being, and both aspects are examined together.
3   What field of investigation is mentioned?
4   What relationship's given between mind and body?
5   How are mind and body examined?

Studies have shown that a continuing state of emotional stress can cause physical changes that lead to disease. The most provocative conclusion that has so far been produced, however, is that different personality types tend to get different diseases.
6   What can cause physical changes?
7   What can these changes lead to?

Some investigators are amassing impressive evidence to show that there is a significant link between the kind of person you are and the kind of bodily disease you are prone to.

8   What are some investigators amassing?
9   What does this evidence show?

The results of a study by the psychiatrist Dr Floyd O. Ring would appear to support the conclusion that 'People with some illnesses can be picked out with a good percentage of accuracy by personality alone.'
   10 What psychiatrist's mentioned?
   11 What does this doctor base his opinions on?
   12 What are some illnesses dependent on?

Further discussion

1   Can you think of any cases of psychosomatic illness among people you know?

2   Taking specific people you know, can you think of what psychosomatic illnesses they might be prone to?

Tobacco is, by definition, a drug.

Outline

Two categories There are two types of drugs
medical
non-medical

Medical While trusted, medical drugs can be a problem

Non-medical Non-medical drugs are related to culture
Some eastern civilizations
reject alcohol due to religion
accept marijuana

Western civilization
accepts alcohol
rejects marijuana
takes tea and coffee

Definition By definition, a drug alters the structure or
function of organisms
some foods
vitamins
air pollutants
tobacco
butter

Ourselves We are all drug-users

What's a drug? Most people probably think there's a perfectly simple answer to this question. In fact, if one conducts a quick survey on any street corner, one finds that, according to the vast majority of people, there are two groups of drugs: those prescribed by doctors, and those which people take for non-medical use. As medicine and the medical profession are generally respected, there aren't any objections to the use of prescribed drugs. What most people don't realize is that although prescribed drugs are usually beneficial, they can also present a serious problem. There weren't many people addicted to tranquillizers before doctors began to prescribe them: now there are literally millions who depend on them.

The acceptance of the use of drugs for non-medical reasons is largely a matter of culture. For example, some Eastern people view the use of alcohol with horror, mainly as a result of religious upbringing. However, these same people freely use marijuana and similar drugs without a second thought, while this, in turn, isn't accepted in a Western culture which accepts alcohol. In most Western societies, the tea- or coffee-break's now a part of life, and huge quantities of these drinks are consumed daily. But these are also a form of drug, since there are stimulating substances contained in both.

A few years ago a drug was defined as any substance which, by its chemical nature, alters the structure or function of the living organism. This definition includes foods, vitamins, air pollutants, and many materials normally present in the body. There's proof now that tobacco in the form of cigarettes is linked with lung cancer. And there's also a definite link between butter, which raises the cholesterol level of the blood, and heart disease – which is the principal health problem in developed countries.

So there aren't any simple definitions for 'drug', and these definitions change from culture to culture. However, if we accept the one just given, we can all describe ourselves as 'drug-users'.

336 words; Difficulty 5

What is a drug? Most people probably think there's a perfectly simple answer to this question. In fact, if one conducts a quick survey on any street corner, one finds that, according to the vast majority of people, there are two groups of drugs: those prescribed by doctors, and those which some people take for non-medical use.

1   How many kinds of drugs are popularly considered to exist?
2   What is the first kind?
3   What is the second kind?

As medicine and the medical profession are generally respected, there aren't any objections to the use of prescribed drugs. What most people don't realize is that, although prescribed drugs are usually beneficial, they can also present a serious problem.

4   Why is there no objection to prescribed drugs?
5   What is the drawback to prescribed drugs?

There weren't many people addicted to tranquillizers before doctors began to prescribe them: now there are literally millions who depend on them.

6   What kind of drug is mentioned?
7   How many people depend on them?

The acceptance of the use of drugs for non-medical reasons is largely a matter of culture. For example, some Eastern people view the use of alcohol with horror, mainly as a result of religious upbringing.

8   On what does the acceptance of drugs for non-medical use largely depend?
9   How do Eastern people view the use of alcohol?
10 What is this attitude the result of?

However, these same people freely use marijuana and similar drugs without a second thought, while this, in turn, is not accepted in a Western culture which accepts alcohol.

11 Which drugs are used in the East?
12 What is the Western view of these?

In most Western societies, the tea- or coffee-break is now a part of life, and huge quantities of these drinks are consumed daily. But these are also a form of drug, since there are stimulating substances contained in both.

13 Which two drugs are mentioned as being common in the West?
14 Why are these considered drugs?

A few years ago a drug was defined as any substance which, by its chemical nature, alters the structure or function of the living organism. This definition includes foods, vitamins, air pollutants, and many materials normally present in the body.

15 How was a drug defined a few years ago?
16 What sort of things does this definition include?

There is proof now that tobacco in the form of cigarettes is linked with lung cancer. And there is also a definite link between butter, which raises the cholesterol level of the blood, and heart disease – which is the principal health problem in developed countries.

17 In what form is tobacco linked with disease?

18 What disease is butter linked with?

19 What effect does butter have on the blood?

So there aren't any simple definitions for 'drug', and these definitions change from culture to culture. However, if we accept the one just given, we can all describe ourselves as 'drug-users'.

20 How do definitions of drugs change?

21 Who can be described as drug-users?

Further discussion

1 Suppose your office considered banning smoking, and you were asked to give your opinions to the personnel association . . .

2 What would you say if a close friend (or a child, or a brother or sister) of yours told you he (or she) had started taking drugs?

3 Surely individuals can decide for themselves what to do with their lives.

4 It seems fairly certain that smoking increases the death rate. What right have people to smoke and endanger, not only themselves, but those who live with them?

5 It's not so much a question of banning drugs, but knowing where to draw the line. Where do you draw the line?

6 It's unintelligent to criticize something if you don't know what's involved. Therefore, any intelligent person should try drugs at least once.

7 Is alcohol a necessity for a smooth social life?

5 Flextime

Outline

Novelty   Flextime is a new development in systems of work
                catching on fast
                spreading

Origin   Flextime started in Germany in the late '60s
                to Britain in 1972

Description Workers start and finish work at will
                all present at key times
                fixed weekly total

Results   The system is a success
                balance between work and home life
                less travel in rush hour
                possibility of finishing a job
                productivity up
                less turnover
                more responsibility

Spreading   Flextime was originally limited to white-collar workers
                applied to manual workers now

A major new development in systems of work in Britain is taking place. Flexible working hours, or 'Flextime', are catching on fast, and this trend is continuing, says the Department of Employment. In 1973, over 500 organizations had adopted the idea, and by 1974, this number had risen to over 200,000.

Flexible working hours were devised in Germany in the late 1960s, but reached Britain only in 1972. The system allows workers to start and finish work whenever they want, with only two provisos. These are, firstly, that all workers must be present for certain 'key' times in the day, and secondly, that all workers must work an agreed total number of hours per week.

The system has proved an almost total success wherever it has been tried. A survey of 700 workers on flexible hours showed three main advantages:
a better balance between working and private life
avoidance of the need to travel during rush hours
and the ability to be able to finish a specific task before leaving.

From the employer's point of view, the system tends to increase productivity, reduce labour turnover and give the workers a greater sense of responsibility. At first, 'Flextime' was mainly confined to white-collar workers, but it is now being successfully applied to manual workers too.

212 words; Difficulty 6

Immediate recall

A major new development in systems of work in Britain is taking place. Flexible working hours, or 'Flextime', are catching on fast, and this trend is continuing, says the Department of Employment.
1   In what area of British life are major changes taking place?
2   What is this new development?
3   Which authority is cited?
4   What does this authority say?

In 1973, over 500 organizations had adopted the idea, and by 1974, this number had risen to over 200,000.
5   How many organizations had adopted 'Flextime' by 1974?

Flexible working hours were devised in Germany in the late 1960s, but only reached Britain in 1972.
6   Where was 'Flextime' developed?
7   When was it developed?
8   When did it reach Britain?

The system allows workers to start and finish work whenever they want, with only two provisos. These are, firstly, that all workers must be present for certain 'key' times in the day, and secondly, that all workers must work an agreed total number of hours per week.

9   What does the system allow workers to do?
10 What is the first proviso?
11 What is the second proviso?

The system has proved an almost total success wherever it has been tried. A survey of 700 workers on flexible hours showed three main advantages:
a better balance between working and private life
avoidance of the need to travel during rush hours
and the ability to be able to finish a specific task before leaving.

12 What sort of success has the scheme had?
13 How has this been demonstrated?
14 How many workers were questioned?
15 What is the first main advantage?
16 What does 'Flextime' help to avoid?
17 How does it help the employee with specific tasks?

From the employer's point of view, the system tends to increase productivity, reduce labour turnover and give the workers a greater sense of responsibility.

18 What effect does the system have on productivity?
19 What does it reduce?
20 What does it give the workers?

At first, 'Flextime' was mainly confined to white-collar workers, but it is now being successfully applied to manual workers too.

21 Which group of workers used 'Flextime' at first?
22 Which group of workers are also using it now?

Further discussion

1   What advantages-disadvantages do you see in 'Flextime'?

2   Do you think people are likely to abuse such a system?

3   What about 'Flextime' in schools? Children must attend a certain number of classes a day . . .

Outline

Conflict   The conflict between youth and our educational system
is serious
  in certain countries
  causes trouble within the educational system
  causes trouble with adult society

Solution   People look to education for help because of
  failure to understand the revolution
  failure to make the revolution unnecessary

Adjustment What must we help adjust to?
  to misery and injustice
  to a narrow existence

Transcript

In certain countries the conflict between young people and the educational system has become very serious indeed. In addition to causing trouble within the educational system itself, the young are also in conflict with the adult society outside it.

In considering how to deal with such issues, many people look to education and to educational institutions for help. This is a natural and understandable response from an older generation that has failed to understand the significance of the revolt of youth and to create a world in which such revolt would be unnecessary.

When we are asked to help in the adjustment of youth, we must ask: 'Adjustment to what?' Should we adjust them, for example, to the miseries and injustices in the world, the hunger and poverty in the midst of plenty? Or do we want them to conform to the comforts of a secure, routine job and a narrow routine existence in a small, closed community?

157 words; Difficulty 6

Immediate recall

In certain countries the conflict between young people and the educational system has become very serious indeed.
  1 What conflict has become very serious?

In addition to causing trouble within the educational system itself, they are also in conflict with the adult society outside it.
  2 What are young people also in conflict with?
  3 What is this conflict in addition to?

In considering how to deal with such issues, many people look to education and to educational institutions for help.
  4 When do people look for help?
  5 What do people look to for help?

This is a natural and understandable response from an older generation that has failed to understand the significance of the revolt of youth and to create a world in which such revolt would be unnecessary.
  6 What sort of a response is this?
  7 What has the older generation failed to understand?
  8 What has the older generation failed to create?

When we are asked to help in the adjustment of youth, we must ask: 'Adjustment to what?'
  9 What must we ask?
  10 When must we ask it?

Should we adjust them, for example, to the miseries and injustices in the world, the hunger and poverty in the midst of plenty?
11 What should we perhaps adjust youth to?
12 What is said to exist in the midst of plenty?

Or do we want them to conform to the comforts of a secure, routine job and a narrow routine existence in a small, closed community?
13 What is it suggested we want youth to conform to?
14 In what sort of community?

Further discussion

1 What must we help youth to adjust to?

2 What is the real conflict with the educational system?

3 To what extent can an older generation adapt to a younger?

4 To what extent is television the cause of delinquency?

5 Is the gap today greater than a generation ago? If so, why?

6 Up to what age should parents have absolute authority over their children?

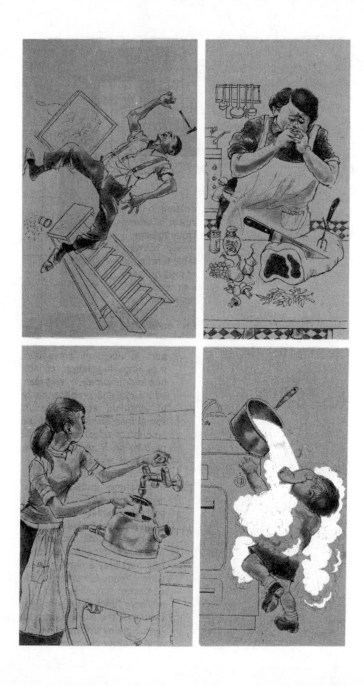

Outline

More machines	In industrialized countries there are more machines every day
Risks	There are several causes of risks Machines are not understood by most people High voltages are involved Kitchen machinery is as dangerous as industrialized
Innovation	There are several reasons for innovation Appearance Novelty Social status

In industrialized countries, the home's rapidly becoming a complicated workshop filled with technically advanced machinery. Some of this machinery's already so complex as to be well beyond the understanding of the persons who have to use it. The resulting accident risks, therefore, are high.

The extent of these risks may be judged from the fact that some new domestic machinery requires the use of very high voltages indeed. In addition, the rotary cutter, common in the kitchen, is capable of a speed well in excess of that of ordinary industrial lathes and drills. It can inflict injuries at least as serious as those produced by an industrial wood-planing machine.

Considerations of necessity and usefulness in design often give way to the less utilitarian arguments of appearance, novelty and even social status. Home mechanization reaches new heights of absurdity with electric toothbrushes (without a grounding wire) and, in the USA, electric erasers.

157 words; Difficulty 6

Immediate recall

In industrialized countries, the home is rapidly becoming a complicated workshop filled with technically advanced machinery.
1   What's the home becoming?
2   Where's this happening?

Some of this machinery is already so complex as to be well beyond the understanding of the persons who have to use it.
3   How does the talk describe modern machinery in the home?
4   What's the result of the complexity of this machinery?

The resulting accident risks, therefore, are high. The extent of these risks may be judged from the fact that some new domestic machinery requires the use of very high voltages indeed.
5   What kind of risks are high?
6   How may the extent of these risks be judged?

In addition, the rotary cutter, common in the kitchen, is capable of a speed well in excess of that of ordinary industrial lathes and drills.
7   Where's the rotary cutter commonly used?
8   What kind of speed's this machine capable of?

It can inflict injuries at least as serious as those produced by an industrial wood-planing machine.
9   How serious are injuries which can be inflicted by the rotary cutter?

Considerations of necessity and usefulness in design often give way to the less utilitarian arguments of appearance, novelty and even social status.

10 Which two considerations are often pushed aside?
11 What are the less utilitarian arguments which these considerations give way to?

Home mechanization reaches new heights of absurdity with electric toothbrushes (without a grounding wire) and, in the USA, electric erasers.

12 With the development of electric toothbrushes, what does home mechanization reach?
13 What problem of electric toothbrushes is mentioned?
14 What other electric device for the home is mentioned as being available in the USA?

Further discussion

1 What other gadgets in the home can you think of?

2 Can you name some of the hazards of the home, and suggest how to avoid them?

3 Can you describe an accident you have had or witnessed in the home? Could it have been avoided?

4 The talk mentions the dangers of high voltage; can you think of situations where this is particularly dangerous? What measures should be taken to avoid such dangerous situations?

Many women now do jobs which used to be carried out exclusively by men.

Outline

Research   Research is being carried out into differences between
men and women
Dr Corinne Hutt
Keele University
Conducting research for several years
Conclusions just published

Development Males and females develop distinctly
Biological predispositions take effect soon
after conception
Social pressures only act from birth

Two sides   Biology and culture both influence development
An understanding of the biological background
helps us to understand the child
shows how certain skills are developed

Biology   Social effects are only partial
Can modify behaviour present for biological
reasons

Transcript

Everyone knows that there are many differences between men and women. Scientists have questioned whether these differences can be expressed in terms of human behaviour, and whether there's a biological basis for them. Dr Corinne Hutt, a professor of psychology at Keele University, has, for some years, been conducting research into these questions, and her conclusions have just been published.

In humans, distinctive male and female development begins soon after conception. From birth onwards, cultural and social pressures act upon the individual, who already has certain predispositions resulting from early hormonal influences. In fact, these influences take effect in the first few weeks after conception.

Dr Hutt's research shows that biology and culture are different aspects of a continuous process of the child's development and growth. By recognizing the biological bases of the child's predispositions, we're able to understand how, as a child develops, it's motivated to behave in some ways, and to reject other forms of behaviour. It also shows how an individual develops certain skills and aptitudes.

Professor Hutt sums up her research with the conclusion that the effect of the social environment on the individual is only partial. It may modify or accentuate certain forms of behaviour already present for biological reasons. Only by acknowledging these two vital aspects can individuals be enabled to fully develop all their possibilities.

224 words; Difficulty 7

Immediate recall

Everyone knows that there are many differences between men and women. Scientists have questioned whether these differences can be expressed in terms of human behaviour, and whether there's a biological basis for them.
1 What's the first question scientists have raised about the differences between men and women?
2 What's the second?

Dr Corinne Hutt, a professor of psychology at Keele University, has, for some years, been conducting research into these questions, and her conclusions have just been published.
3 Who's mentioned?
4 What's she been studying?
5 What's just been published?

In humans, distinctive male and female development begins soon after conception. From birth onwards, cultural and social pressures act upon the individual, who already has certain predispositions resulting from early hormonal influences. In fact, these influences take effect in the first few weeks after conception.

6 What begins soon after conception in humans?
7 What happens to the individual from birth onwards?
8 What does the individual already have at birth?
9 What causes these predispositions?
10 When do these influences take effect?

Dr Hutt's research shows that biology and culture are different aspects of a continuous process of the child's development and growth.

11 What does Dr Hutt's research demonstrate about the relationship between biology and culture?

By recognizing the biological bases of the child's predispositions, we are able to understand how, as a child develops, it is motivated to behave in some ways, and to reject other forms of behaviour. It also shows how an individual develops certain skills and aptitudes.

12 What should be recognized?
13 What are we able to understand as a result of this?
14 What other aspects of individual development are mentioned?

Professor Hutt sums up her research with the conclusion that the effect of the social environment on the individual is only partial. It may modify or accentuate certain forms of behaviour already present for biological reasons. Only by acknowledging these two vital aspects can individuals be enabled to fully develop all their possibilities.

15 What's the conclusion of Professor Hutt's research?
16 How does the social environment alter certain forms of behaviour?
17 What must be acknowledged?
18 What can individuals then be enabled to do?

Further discussion

1 'Until men regularly give birth to children, the idea that men and women can be equal is a myth.' (Herodotus)

2 Inequality is not unjust. Why do people make such a 'thing' about equality?

3 An employer would not give an equal chance to two candidates for a job if one said that, every so often, he went on holiday for three months. Why should he give an equal chance to a man and a woman if the woman risks having a child and stopping work for a few months or even longer?
   While having children and going on holiday are not the same thing, both are normally the result of a voluntary decision.

4 After the appearance of the Equal Rights Act made discrimination illegal in Britain, this advertisement appeared in a newspaper:
   Wanted: Secretary/receptionist, good typing/shorthand, man or woman, preferably with a figure resembling Miss World's.
   Comment.

The population explosion.

Outline

Increase   The population increase is staggering
                    1,000 million in 1840
                    2,000 million in 1930
                    3,000 million in 1960
                    6,000 million before 2000

Developed countries   In highly developed countries the increase has slowed

Developing countries   In developing countries it is unchecked

Result of malnutrition   Malnutrition is related to population growth
                    People are not sure children will survive
                    People are reluctant to limit their families
                    Can hold up economic development

Result of development   Economic development results in limited families

Transcript

The increases in world population projected for the decades immediately ahead are staggering. It took from the beginning of man to about 1840 for world population to reach the first thousand million, then only about a hundred years for the second, and the third thousand million mark was reached in 1960, after an interval of only thirty years. Regardless of any future effectiveness of family planning efforts, world population seems certain to reach six thousand million by the end of this century or soon after.

While the rate of increase has slowed or even stabilized in most of the highly developed countries, it is continuing unchecked in those places least prepared to cope with it in terms of either food supply or other resources.

Two of the world's most pressing problems, malnutrition and rapid population growth, are intimately related. Malnutrition is, in fact, the major determinant of the high death rates. At the same time, people are apparently reluctant to limit the size of their families until they are assured that the majority of their children will survive.

Both these factors can hold up the process of social and economic development, though paradoxically this very development could provide an incentive to individual couples to limit the number of their children. In the highly industrialized countries, the desire to limit family size has been a consequence of improved economic and social opportunity.

230 words; Difficulty 7

Immediate recall

The increases in world population projected for the decades immediately ahead are staggering.
1   What's said to be staggering?
2   What period of time's mentioned?

It took from the beginning of man to about 1840 for world population to reach the first thousand million, then only about a hundred years for the second, and the third thousand million mark was reached in 1960, after an interval of only thirty years.
3   What does the year 1840 mark?
4   About when did world population reach two thousand million?
5   When did it reach the three thousand million mark?

Regardless of any future effectiveness of family planning efforts, world population seems certain to reach six thousand million by the end of this century or soon after.
6   When will world population reach the six thousand million mark?
7   In what areas are measures being taken?

While the rate of increase has slowed or even stabilized in most of the highly developed countries, it is continuing unchecked in those places least prepared to cope with it in terms of either food supply or other resources.

8 Where has the rate of increase slowed or even stabilized?
9 Where's the rate of increase of population still unchecked?
10 In what ways are those places least prepared?

Two of the world's most pressing problems, malnutrition and rapid population growth, are intimately related. Malnutrition is, in fact, the major determinant of the high death rates.

11 What are two of the world's most pressing problems?
12 What is, in fact, malnutrition the major determinant of?

At the same time, people are apparently reluctant to limit the size of their families until they are assured that the majority of their children will survive.

13 What are people apparently reluctant to do?
14 What assurance do they need?

Both these factors can hold up the process of social and economic development, though paradoxically this very development could provide an incentive to individual couples to limit the number of their children.

15 What are malnutrition and population growth said to affect?
16 What could this development provide?

In the highly industrialized countries, the desire to limit family size has been a consequence of improved economic and social opportunity.

17 What has the desire to limit family size been the consequence of?

Further discussion

1 What right have we to increase world population?

2 What obligation have we to adopt, where possible, children from overpopulated countries?

3 What measures can governments of overpopulated countries take, morally, to limit the population?

4 Help to developing countries is the reason that natural means for limiting population are no longer effective.

5 Medicine contributes to a larger population, which in turn aggravates medical problems.

6 The population of the world could be twelve thousand million in 2040. Imagine the political implication of this.

7 The increase in world population is the greatest revolution that mankind is likely to meet within the next generation.

The family provides a domestic context for children.

Outline

Domestic context	Every society must provide a domestic context for children.
Definition of family	The word 'family' has two meanings Parents and children Relations
Wife junior	The wife is presumed the junior partner Wife's career fits the husband's Children's dependence is exploited
Dispersion	Families become scattered Wife can't ask family to help
Ideals	We have three ideals that can't co-exist Social equality of men and women Permanence of marriage Lifelong love and cooperation between parents and children
Problem	Is the family possible?

As human children are unusually dependent for an unusually long time, it's obvious that every society must provide a domestic context in which the children are brought up and educated.

The problem, however, is that we assume that the family, in the sense of a domestic household, ought to be the same as the family considered as parents and children.

In present day English, the word 'family' has two meanings: firstly, the domestic group of parents and children; and secondly, a network of relations, for example, the set of people who might be expected to turn up at a wedding or a funeral. At the first level, my brothers and sisters and myself are all in the same family as children, but in different ones as parents; but at the second level, we're all in the same family from start to finish.

Despite some modifications over the last century, the wife is still presumed to be very much the junior partner in a marriage. It's normally the wife's career that has to be reshaped to fit the husband's, not the other way round. The dependence of children on their mother is exploited in a wholly unreasonable way to make the wife-mother the slave of the household. This is all tied up with the fact that, in our industrial system, job-changing and commuting tends to scatter the members of a family, and the harassed wife-mother finds it more and more difficult to rely on her relations for practical assistance.

As nuclear families become more isolated, families of relations become more dispersed. The young mother can still talk to her Mum on the phone, but she can't ask her to drop in for a few minutes to watch the baby. Ideas about the status of women have been changing: wives are thought to be the companions of their husbands rather than their slaves. But perhaps they're more thoroughly enslaved to their children than before.

The point is that there doesn't seem to be any solution. There's a genuine clash between the right of the woman to be treated as a free and self-respecting individual, and the right of the child to demand care and attention. We have created for ourselves three ideals: social equality of men and women; permanence of the marriage; and lifelong love and co-operation between parents and children. However, we have created a social system in which it's quite impossible for these factors to co-exist.

It is not so much, then, a question of whether the family's a necessity, but whether it's at all possible.

434 words; Difficulty 7

Immediate recall

As human children are unusually dependent for an unusually long time, it's obvious that every society must provide a domestic context in which the children are brought up and educated.
1   What must every society provide for its children?
2   Why must society provide this?

The problem, however, is that we assume that the family, in the sense of a domestic household, ought to be the same as the family considered as parents and children.
3   What problem's mentioned?

In present day English, the word 'family' has two meanings: firstly, the domestic group of parents and children; and secondly, a network of relations, for example, the set of people who might be expected to turn up at a wedding or a funeral.
4   How many meanings has the word 'family' in present day English?
5   What's the first level of meaning?
6   What's the second level?

At the first level, my brothers and sisters and myself are all in the same family as children, but in different ones as parents; but at the second level, we are all in the same family from start to finish.
7   Who belongs to the family at the first level of meaning?
8   Who belongs to it at the second level?

Despite some modifications over the last century, the wife is still presumed to be very much the junior partner in a marriage. It is normally the wife's career that has to be reshaped to fit the husband's, not the other way round.
9   When have modifications taken place?
10 What's the wife's role in marriage considered to be?
11 Whose career's normally reshaped to fit the other's?

The dependence of children on their mother is exploited in a wholly unreasonable way, to make the wife-mother the slave of the household.
12 What's said about the dependence of children on their mother?
13 What's the result of this?

This is all tied up with the fact that, in our industrial system, job-changing and commuting tends to scatter the members of a family, and the harassed wife-mother finds it more and more difficult to rely on her relations for practical assistance.
14 What tends to happen to the members of a family in our industrial system?
15 What effect does this have on the wife-mother?

As nuclear families become more isolated, families of relations become more dispersed. The young mother can still talk to her mum on the phone, but she can't ask her to drop in for a few minutes to watch the baby.

16 What kind of families are becoming more dispersed?

17 As a result, what's the relationship of a young mother with her own mother?

Ideas about the status of women have been changing: wives are thought to be the companions of their husbands rather than their slaves. But perhaps they are more thoroughly enslaved to their children than before.

18 What's been changing?

19 What's the role of wives now thought to be?

20 What's their present relationship with their children?

The point is that there doesn't seem to be any solution. There is a genuine clash between the right of the woman to be treated as a free and self-respecting individual, and the right of the child to demand care and attention.

21 What seems to be the problem?

22 What right of the woman is mentioned?

23 What does this clash with?

We have created for ourselves three ideals: social equality of men and women; permanence of the marriage; and lifelong love and co-operation between parents and children. However, we have created a social system in which it is quite impossible for these three factors to co-exist.

It is not so much, then, a question of whether the family is a necessity, but whether it is at all possible.

24 Ideally, what should be the status of men and women?

25 How long should parents and children love and co-operate with each other?

26 What's the drawback of the social system which we have created?

Further discussion

1 In some northern countries, housing estates have central restaurants and nurseries in order to take the load off the mothers. Can you suggest any ways, in your immediate surroundings, of modifying our social system in order to help solve the problem?

2 What advantages and disadvantages are involved in raising children as members of a community rather than as members of a family?

3 We have three ideals that can not co-exist. In order to keep the situation of the family unchanged, which of these ideals would you be prepared to sacrifice?

4 To what extent do boarding schools solve the problem?

Further practice

Any recorded talk gives practice in shadowing on condition it is spoken with few or no pauses, and on condition you stay at least three seconds behind the speaker.

You can also buy records of spoken English which give further practice.

Part 2   Outline writing

In order to recall the content of a talk, the listener must be active mentally organizing the information he's receiving. To do this, he must: get the central ideas,
   separate central and secondary ideas,
   separate relevant and irrelevant information.

In Part 1, each talk was accompanied by an outline. In this Part, you will be given systematic training in writing outlines on your own.

Finding the central idea

Listen to each of the extracts, and choose the central idea from the four that are given in your book. The transcripts and the answers are on pages 53–55.

11

a Overeating causes overweight.
b Overeating is hereditary.
c Exercise prevents overweight.
d People who eat a lot don't get much exercise.

12

a The completion of the Panama Canal was delayed by disease.
b Workers on the Panama Canal brought yellow fever from China.
c The route of the Panama Canal lies across swamp and jungle.
d Both yellow fever and malaria are carried by mosquitoes.

13

a People live longer in the USSR.
b Retaining authority in the family is one of the most important requirements for a long life.
c The oldest person in the world is 165.
d Active people live longer.

14

a All human communities train soldiers to kill.
b Humans are not aggressive by instinct.
c Every large community has an army.
d Everyone is violent.

15

a The best method of teaching swimming is by imitation.
b Small babies can learn to swim.
c Babies can learn to swim on condition they are very small.
d It only takes fifteen to twenty lessons to teach a child to swim.

16

a The road accident rate is increasing.
b Road accidents are mainly limited to technically developed countries.
c As a result of road accidents, many more people are disabled than are killed.
d Road accidents present the most common cause of death.

17

a Different people see things in different ways.
b Pleasant things are seen quickly.
c Unpleasant things are denied.
d Differences in perception are a delusion.

18

a South America is a major exporter of potatoes.
b Only a few people in South America benefit from food exchanges.
c South American food products have a lower nutritional value than European products.
d South America imports food from Europe.

Transcripts and solutions (11–18)

11

Overeating causes overweight; yet more important than the large amount of food may be the small amount of exercise. In other words, if you want to eat a lot, take a lot of exercise. In some cases, heredity may also be a factor.

c.

12

During the building of the Panama Canal in the 1880's, thousands upon thousands of labourers, most of them brought from China, died of yellow fever. The seventy-five kilometres of the Canal's route lay across swamp and jungle, an ideal breeding-ground for mosquitoes. Between them, yellow fever and malaria claimed so many victims that work had to be abandoned and the Canal was finally opened only in 1914.

a.

13

Generally speaking, people who live in the countryside and work continuously from their youth till the end of their lives last the longest. In the USSR, there is a man aged 165 and another aged 130. Both still work as much as they can on the land. They also still have authority and status in the family and the community. Specialists believe this to be one of the most important requirements for a long life.

d.

14

We observe that most large human communities up until now have trained whole groups of men, such as soldiers, to kill. Nevertheless, there is no basis for speaking of a human 'aggressive instinct'. Almost any human being can be provoked to violence, but no internal force has been discovered which demands that each person perform his quota of violent acts.

b.

15

Some children learn to swim, before they can talk, by imitation. The teacher demonstrates breathing, for example, by opening his mouth and raising his head, then closing his mouth and putting his head under a little way. Even very young babies can be taught by this method. Usually, it takes about fifteen to twenty lessons, though exceptional children can learn in less.
b.

16

Deaths from road accidents increase every year in nearly all the technically developed countries. Many people escape death, but remain disabled, condemned to spend the rest of their lives in a hospital or a home, or to be dependent on their relatives. In a few years from now, it's expected that there will be a quarter of million deaths in the world, and ten million serious injuries, due to road accidents every year.
a.

17

People see things differently. Even 'facts' may be seen differently by different people. Relevance to one's needs is the most important determinant of one's personal view of the world. For instance, things that seem to be aids to satisfying one's needs are seen quickly. But things that look like obstacles may also be seen quickly, only then to be denied, so that they appear not to have been seen at all.
a.

People see things differently.

18

Food exchanges between continents generally bring advantages, but there are exceptions. South America, throughout its history, has exported basics such as potatoes and maize, yet the wheat and milk it imports from Europe, of much higher food value, are available only to a privileged few.
b.

Finding the central idea

In this exercise you will hear a further four texts (19–22). Once again, you are asked for the central idea of each. This time you will have no help, so close your books. The Transcripts and Solutions are below.

Transcripts and solutions (19–22)

19

Mankind is always searching for a better life. One way of improving it is to plan work so that it corresponds to the capacities and needs of the worker. Ergonomics is concerned with fitting work to man. It doesn't limit its goal to the elimination of physical hazards to health, but aims at making the work more satisfying to the worker.

Work can be organized to suit man's capabilities.

20

Man has added extraneous substances to his food since prehistoric times. Salt and spices are the oldest food additives we know of, used by prehistoric man to preserve his meat and fish, and to make the taste more interesting. Today, the substances, natural and synthetic, added to food run into thousands. Most of the foods we buy contain one or more additives.

Most food nowadays contains additives.

21

It is not necessary to emphasize the enormous restrictions that blindness imposes upon the ordinary procedures of earning a living: we're only too well aware that we're in general more dependent on sight than on smell, touch or hearing. But it's worth pointing out that sight affects the knowledge of the world we receive through our other senses.

We are dependent on sight.

22

In most developing countries, two-thirds or more of the people live in rural areas, with few, if any, of the services the city-dweller takes for granted. Water taps in houses, for example, are almost unknown. At best, there may be a village well. Often the only source of water is a lake or a stream, perhaps several kilometres away. The drudgery of water-carrying can take up the better part of every day.

Most people in developing countries have to carry all their water.

Rephrasing the speaker's words (23–29)

When you state the main idea of a text, you can understand much better if you use your own words. Suppose, for instance, that a speaker says:

'There is a tendency to a positive correlation between quality and cost in the case of the produce of our better restaurants.'

We could rephrase this as: 'Good restaurants tend to cost more.'

In the next exercise you are asked to rephrase a number of statements using your own words. You should try to rephrase each statement in as many ways as you can.

Listen to each short extract as many times as you like. The transcripts and suggested answers are on pages 57 and 58.

Transcripts and solutions (23–29)

23

There is a tendency to a positive correlation between quality and cost in the case of the produce of our better restaurants.

The following are possible answers:

Good restaurants tend to cost more.
Good food is expensive.
Expensive restaurants are better than cheap ones.
You have to pay for good quality food.
If you want to eat well, you have to pay a lot.
You can eat the best food in expensive restaurants.

24

Despite certain similarities, patterns of work for agricultural workers vary considerably from one part of the world to another.

The following are possible answers:

Farmers in different countries have different work.
There is a big difference between the farm work round the world.
Types of farm work vary according to the part of the world.
Farm work is different in different countries.

25

If a large number of people in different places is taken into consideration, it will be seen that the overall time spent sleeping each night, in response to physical demands, is in the order of eight hours.

The following are possible answers:

The average human sleeps for eight hours a night.
Most people need eight hours sleep daily.
The average person needs to sleep for eight hours each day.

26

We cannot avoid recognizing that a certain amount of training is necessary to understand pictures, for it is only too clear that many of us do not understand many types of pictorial art.

The following are possible answers:

We have to learn how to understand pictures.
Understanding pictures has to be learned.

Training is necessary to understand painting.
Paintings can't be understood without some training.
An untrained person can't understand pictures.
People who lack training can't understand paintings.

27

An individual whose economic situation is sufficiently weak as to find himself totally without personal finance will inevitably discover that it is necessary to possess liquid funds in order to purchase essentials such as nourishment and habitation.

The following are possible answers:

You need money to survive.
If you're too poor, you can't buy anything.
Money is necessary.
Food and shelter aren't free.
Money doesn't grow on trees.
You need money for the basic things in life.
You can't get something for nothing.

28

Physical discomfort caused by a lowering of atmospheric temperature is easily circumvented by the addition of thicker wearing apparel.

The following are possible answers:

Warm clothes keep out the cold.
Put on woollen jumpers in winter.
Wear woollen clothes to keep warm.
If you want to keep warm, put on extra thick clothes.
When it's cold outside, wear your warmest clothes.

29

It is of considerable importance, in order to avoid physical hazard, that all members of the population should exercise maximum precautions in urban situations with regard to vehicles in motion.

The following are possible answers:

Look out when crossing the road.
Traffic is dangerous in towns.
Be careful when walking along the street.
Busy traffic can be dangerous.
Look both ways before crossing the street.
Take care to avoid fast-moving cars.
In town, keep your eyes open for the traffic.

Separating central and secondary ideas (30–33)

Once we have the central idea of a talk, we must discover the secondary ideas.

In the following four talks you are asked to choose, from the lists below, the idea which you consider is central to each. You should write this down in your notebook. Under this, and slightly indented, you should write the secondary ideas. Your answers will look something like this:

> Restaurants are becoming more expensive.
>> Food is more expensive.
>> Wages are higher.
>> More people prefer to eat at home.

30

American speech communities have constantly mixed.
Bigger pronunciation differences exist in England than in the States.
American families have been constantly on the move.
The three American dialects differ very little.

31

Short things are easier to remember than long.
Familiar things are easier to remember than unfamiliar.
Some things are easy to remember.
Interesting things are easier to remember than dull.

32

Small scissors tend to have small holes.
Scissors are now made with holes to fit hands.
Ergonomic scissors are a success.
Scissors for left-handed people have a red handle.

33

Water drunk in the morning.
Water drunk during the day.
Water is vital for the body.
Water between meals.
Water to clean the body.

30

In spite of countless smaller variations in pronunciation, vocabulary and idiom, the three American dialects don't greatly differ. For three centuries, American families have been constantly on the move, and speech communities have seldom remained isolated for more than one generation. It would be no exaggeration to say that greater differences in pronunciation are discernible in the north of England between Trent and Tweed than in the whole of North America.

The three American dialects differ very little
    American families have been constantly on the move
    American speech communities have constantly mixed
    Bigger pronunciation differences exist in England than in the States

31

Some things are easy to remember. A short poem is easier to memorize than a long one; an interesting story is better recalled than a dull one. But brevity and wit are not all that is involved. Equally important is the way things fit together. If a new task meshes well with what we have previously learned, our earlier learning can be transferred with profit to the novel situation. If not, the task is that much harder to master.

Some things are easy to remember
    Short things are easier to remember than long
    Interesting things are easier to remember than dull
    Familiar things are easier to remember than unfamiliar

32

Start your day by drinking a couple of glasses of water, and drink at least six to eight glasses more during the rest of the day. Water is absolutely vital for the body to function properly and water – not soft drinks, coffee, tea or alcohol – is the best drink for between meals. Water also helps to clean the body. If you can, you should take a daily shower or bath.

Water is vital for the body
    Water drunk in the morning
    Water drunk during the day
    Water between meals
    Water to clean the body

33

There are scissors large and small. For a long time it was customary to design the small ones as copies on a reduced scale of the 'normal-sized' ones. The holes for the fingers became smaller, but the fingers didn't. A few years ago, a manufacturer had the novel idea of introducing a pair of scissors designed to fit the hand. These ergonomic scissors found their market very soon. There was only one complaint; they didn't fit the left hand. Now, the left-handed also have their own pair, with a red handle.

Scissors are now made with holes to fit hands
    Small scissors tend to have small holes
    Ergonomic scissors are a success
    Scissors for left-handed people have a red handle

Separating relevant and irrelevant material (34–38)

In the next five extracts you are asked to choose, from a list, the central idea. You are also asked to choose, from the same list, those ideas which you consider as relevant secondary points, and to reject those ideas you consider irrelevant. Not all the ideas are sufficiently relevant to be classified as secondary.

34

Improvements in eating habits have increased the average height of adults.
Rich people eat better than poor people.
Children who eat well have a better chance of growing taller.
The average height of European adults increases by 10 cm every century.
In Europe, each generation is about $2\frac{1}{2}$ cm taller than the last.
On average, poor children are shorter than rich ones.
The difference continues into adult life.

35

Washington did his job well.
Washington never travelled to Europe.
Washington was different from other presidents of his time.
Washington's studies were considered insufficient for a man in his position.
Washington had very little formal education.
Washington felt his inability to speak directly to foreigners would be embarrassing.

36

A pilot can consider the prevailing weather conditions.
A person flying a plane can do a lot to help himself.
A pilot can fly at a speed and on a course best suited to his machine.
A pilot flying a plane can't stop his engines before he lands.

37

The goal of worldwide eradication of smallpox seems within reach.
Smallpox was declared eradicated from the Americas in 1973.
Smallpox only occurs regularly in four countries now.
Smallpox is endemic in three countries in Asia and one in Africa.
A commission in Brazil discussed the disease.
A special commission concluded the disease has been eliminated from the western hemisphere.
Not a single case was detected in the Americas after 1971.

38

If a student wants to understand 100% of everything, he won't advance.
Everyone must understand in order to speak.
A student who wants to understand 100% of everything will advance slowly.
It isn't necessary to understand 100% of everything we hear.

Transcripts and solutions (34–38)

34

If you eat well when you're a child, you've a better chance of growing taller. Improvements in eating habits during the last 100 years have increased the average height of adults. Even in Europe, each generation is about $2\frac{1}{2}$ cm taller than the last. This means an increase of 10 cm every century.

Since rich people eat better than poor people, the children of poor parents are, on average, shorter than those of rich ones. The difference continues into adult life.

Children who eat well have a better chance of growing taller.
> Improvements in eating habits have increased the average height of adults.
> In Europe, each generation is about $2\frac{1}{2}$ cm taller than the last.
> On average, poor children are shorter than rich ones.

35

George Washington differed from other American presidents of his time mainly in that he'd very little formal education. His studies, in fact, were considered quite insufficient for a man in his position. Nevertheless, he did his job well, though he never travelled to Europe, as he felt that his inability to speak directly to foreign diplomats would be too embarrassing.

George Washington was different from other presidents of his time.
> His studies were considered insufficient for a man in his position.
> He felt his inability to speak directly to foreigners would be embarrassing.
> He never travelled to Europe.

36

After a pilot has left the ground in a plane, he cannot stop his engines before he lands again – unless he wants to kill himself. However, there's a lot he can do voluntarily to help himself. For example, he can fly at a speed and on a course best suited to his machine under the prevailing weather conditions.

A pilot flying a plane can't stop his engines before he lands.
He can do a lot to help himself.
He can take the prevailing weather conditions into consideration.
He can fly at a speed and on a course best suited to his machine.

37

Smallpox was declared eradicated from the Americas in 1973. Not a single case had been detected anywhere on the continent since 1971, and a special commission convened in Brazil concluded that the disease has been eliminated from the entire western hemisphere. Smallpox occurs regularly in only four countries now, three in Asia and one in Africa. The ultimate goal of worldwide eradication seems at last within reach.

The goal of worldwide eradication of smallpox seems within reach.
A special commission concluded the disease has been eliminated from the western hemisphere.
Smallpox only occurs regularly in four countries now.

38

Everyone must understand in order to speak. However, it is not necessary to understand 100% of everything we hear. On the contrary. If a student wants to understand 100% of everything, he'll never advance. Or at least he'll advance very slowly.

Everyone must understand in order to speak.
It isn't necessary to understand 100% of everything we hear.

Transcripts and solutions (39–43)

In the next five extracts you should write down the central idea. You should also write down those ideas which you consider to be relevant secondary points. This time you'll have no help in the form of a list.

39

The child who learns his first language has somehow, we don't understand how, succeeded in inventing for himself an underlying system of abstract processes in language that he puts to use in producing and interpreting the endless variety of structures that constitutes the normal flow of speech. Furthermore, he creates other novel utterances on the appropriate occasions, and understands when he encounters them.

A child creates an abstract language system and uses it
    to understand novel utterances
    to create novel utterances.

40

A learner is said to perform overtly when his performance is observable. If a learner asks a question in the language he's learning, he is performing overtly. If he repeats something, once again his performance is overt. The learner can, however, perform covertly by simply thinking the question or the repetition. Covert activity is, by definition, unobservable.

Performance can be either overt or covert.
    Overt activity is observable.
    Covert activity is unobservable.

41

When we listen to music at home in the evening, there are a number of other things going on at the same time: the noise of traffic in the street; the neighbours; the hum of the fridge . . . Each of these is what's called a peripheral stimulus. We are normally unaware of peripheral stimuli, unless something changes one of them suddenly. So, if the fridge suddenly stops, we are aware of a sudden sense of relief, though we may not know why.

Peripheral stimuli surround us.
    We are unaware of them.
    We become aware if one changes.

42

Aggressiveness, a characteristic associated largely with men though not confined to them, is exciting and addictive. In primitive societies, killing people was the only thing not considered the work of both sexes – men were always the fighters. The pacifist influence of women, therefore, could provide the brake we need against mob violence, war and world destruction.

The pacifist influence of women could be essential to world peace.
Aggressiveness is exciting and addictive.
It is largely associated with men.

43

To ask a language student, after twenty hours of course, to converse about his job or studies would be unrealistic, though we might expect such a student to introduce himself and say where he works, lives or studies and what he does. Furthermore, to ask any student, at any level, to converse on anything as well as a native speaker is again, in most circumstances, unrealistic.

We must be realistic in what we ask students to do.
After 20 hours, a student can't discuss his job or studies.
At any level, he probably can't converse as well as a native speaker.

Further Practice

Any recording of one paragraph of a text will give you further practice.

Part 3

Practice in simultaneous note-taking I

The following is a summary of the note-taking process.

1　Use only one side of loose-leaf notebook paper.

2　Draw a margin eight centimetres from the left-hand side of the page, and then another ten centimetres from the left-hand side. This will give you two lines two centimetres apart.

3　Write main ideas to the right of the first margin. Each main idea should be a complete statement.

4　Write secondary ideas to the right of the second margin.

5　Use abbreviations, but only standard abbreviations, and be sure you can work them out a few months later.

6　Rephrase ideas in your own words. Only use the speaker's words if these have meaning for you.

7　After completing the notes on the right-hand side of the margin, go back reading and deciding which are the main points. Place labels, not statements or the same words as the right side, in the left-hand column to give clues as to the material on the right.

8　Pile your sheets of paper with the first at the bottom, overlapping each other so that only the part in the left-hand column shows. Then go over your notes making an active effort to reconstruct the talk mentally. Whenever you are not sure, check by looking at the notes to the right of the margin.

In the following exercises:

1　Write simultaneous outlines for the recordings.

2　Shadow each recording.

3　Reconstruct each extract from your outline; first orally, and then in writing.

44 Minamata Bay

In 1953 cases of an unknown nervous disease were recorded among animals in the area around Minamata Bay in Kyushu, Japan. The first cases of this disease among humans were noted in 1956. Among the symptoms, which were all serious nervous disorders, were such things as blindness, stupor and convulsions.

It was then observed that all these cases were among families who depended very heavily on sea-food. After much investigation, the trouble was finally traced to polluted water. A factory beside the bay had dumped chemical waste into it. This had been eaten by fish, which in turn were eaten by humans, and this is what caused the disease.

When the extent of the problem became public, there was a great outcry. People wanted guarantees that there would be no more pollution; they wanted compensation for the victims; and they wanted those responsible to be punished.

None of this helped the victims. Mercury compounds accumulate in the body, and the damage they cause to the central nervous system is usually irreversible.

171 words; Difficulty 7

Further discussion

1 Everyone talks about pollution, but no-one seems to do anything. What can each individual do to help?

2 What sanctions can be given to industry for causing pollution?

3 How many different examples of pollution can you think of?

45 Modern Language Teaching

While more people than ever before are learning foreign languages in public and private institutions, there are three striking sources of inefficiency in modern teaching.

First, while language provides a means of saying and doing things, teaching is generally divorced from the use we make of language. We teach an unapplied system, rather than teaching students directly to do things that they need to do through language.

Second, language is a social tool used by thinking social individuals. Nevertheless, we teach students to do and say things with language which are fundamentally insignificant to them as persons, and consequently they say these things formally and impersonally.

A third great source of inefficiency is due to an effort to teach all the students in a group at the same rate. We acknowledge that this is unfair to the capable student, but we probably don't realize the unfairness to the slow student, who's often taken as being unintelligent. There's no evidence that slow students are necessarily unintelligent, or that unintelligent students are incapable of learning a language.

With properly designed courses, students, free to move at their own normal rate, learning to do what they need to with the language, while committing themselves as persons, can rise to unprecedented levels of competence.

212 words; Difficulty 4

Further discussion

1 Language teaching can be improved. How could other subjects studied at school be improved?

2 Language teaching programmes often depend on final examinations. What advantages and disadvantages do you see to examinations?

3 How could examinations for various subjects be improved?

4 What arguments can you think of which would justify the adoption of Esperanto by the United Nations?

46 Slums

A walk through any of the city slums in the developing world is a depressing experience. Such slums usually start just outside the city limits. As they are peopled largely by those attracted to the possibility of finding work and better living conditions in the city, they grow at an amazing speed. A slum, therefore, very quickly develops a communal life, but it also develops problems.

Slum dwellers usually live in huts, which are built of anything that's available . . . planks of wood, sacking, even pieces of metal such as the hub caps of cars. The floor is simply hard mud which, in the cramped conditions, attracts all kinds of disease-carrying insects.

There are no toilets, and the water supply, with a bit of luck, may be one single tap a long walk away. In extreme cases, it may simply be a water hole used by animals and humans alike. There are no health services and no schools. There's no effective public transport service, and the long journey time involved usually prevents the slum population from benefiting from any improvement schemes arranged by the city authorities.

More than 1,000 million people throughout the world live in inadequate housing. To all the obvious health hazards this produces, we must add the psychological and social problems of over-crowding, insecurity, family instability and crime.

221 words; Difficulty 5

Further discussion

1 Are there any slums in the capital city of your country? Why, or why not?

2 Slums seemed to be caused by people who are attracted to big cities. How can this be avoided?

47 An International Language

Before the sixteenth century, there was no real problem about a common language for Europe; for scholars, at least, it was Latin. But after 1870, French, which had taken over as the dominant language, began to lose its place as the most important of the European languages.

In the late nineteenth century, two attempts were made to develop an international language. The first was Volapük or 'Worldspeak', invented by a German priest, J. M. Schleyer, in 1880. This was based on a kind of English. It was a huge success, but was quickly forgotten.

Esperanto, which succeeded Volapük, was much more famous. However, optimism has dropped since the last war – partly because of the new importance of Asian and African languages, which give less hope for world languages based on European roots. It might also be partly due to the increasing importance of the Americans, who, in general, have very little enthusiasm for learning another language. However, Esperantists still make up a loyal international club.

A correspondent in Yorkshire, England, writes: 'There is a camaraderie and brotherhood among Esperantists of all nations which is what's needed throughout the world among all peoples.'

192 words; Difficulty 5

Further discussion

1   What advantages and disadvantages do you see to an international language?

2   What is to prevent English becoming an international language?

3   It has been said that Great Britain and the United States are separated by a common language. How would you explain this statement, and do you agree?

48   Is Schizophrenia Hereditary?

Mainly because mental illness tends to run in families, people have long believed that it is hereditary. However, some psychologists pointed out that, as children are directly influenced by the way they are raised, mental illness might easily run in families simply because of the effect disturbed parents have on their children.

However, the results of two investigations seem to prove conclusively that schizophrenia, at least, is inherited. Firstly, this disorder was not found to exist much more frequently in both identical (one-egg) twins than in both fraternal (two-egg) twins. After this experiment, critics said that this could easily be the case because parents would automatically treat identical twins differently.

The second investigation involved checking people who had been Adopted in infancy and who'd later been hospitalized for schizophrenia. It was found that schizophrenia was concentrated in the biological families, but it occurred with only average frequency in the adoptive families. This proved decisively that schizophrenia is, in fact, inherited.

160 words; Difficulty 6

Further discussion

1   What other character traits do you think are environmental, and what hereditary?

2   Bach and Mozart came from families of musicians. Can you think of other examples of famous people and people you know who were influenced by their family's interests?

3   What constitutes a 'normal' person?

Practice in simultaneous note-taking II

The next three talks are short lectures lasting 4 or 5 minutes each. The following pages give, for each:
   the title,
   the transcript.
Before you listen to each lecture.
   look at the title.
      write down six sentences stating what you think the main points in each talk will be.
As you listen to each lecture:
   take notes.
When you have finished: look over your notes.
   listen to the talk again, and check your outline.
   shadow the talk.

49   Ecumenopolis – A World City

'The open question is not whether Ecumenopolis is going to come into existence: it is whether its maker, mankind, is going to be its master or its victim.' *Arnold Toynbee* in *Cities on the Move*

Originally cities were built on a small scale, the scale of the pedestrian; thus third millennium B.C. Ur resembled eighteenth century Weimar. The cities served the same limited purposes – trade and government centres for agricultural communities – and were similar in development and restricted in size, the overwhelming majority of the world's population being rural.

But now mechanized cities have come into being and scale is no longer of great importance. Furthermore, the mechanized cities are not stationary, but are joining together to form megalopoles. The outstanding example today is the conurbation extending from Boston through New York, Philadelphia and Baltimore to Washington D.C., along the north-eastern seaboard of the United States. Moreover, this north-eastern seaboard megalopolis and a Great Lakes megalopolis are beginning to join. 'The megalopoles on all the continents,' says Toynbee, 'are merging to form Ecumenopolis, a new type of city that can be represented by only one specimen, since Ecumenopolis is going to . . . encompass the land-surface of the globe with a single conurbation.'

The population of the cities is growing at an even faster rate than the population of the world as a whole. People are leaving rural areas and flocking to the cities – in underdeveloped countries because there are no prospects on the land, and in developed countries because increased mechanization has made vast numbers of workers redundant.

An important size factor is the density of the cities, which is lower than of pre-Industrial Revolution days owing to the proliferation of residential suburbias consisting of low houses surrounded by gardens, creating enormous villa cities: Melbourne, Australia and Tokyo, Japan for example. Thus the urbanized area of the planet is increasing rapidly.

Toynbee predicts that the European megalopolis will extend from the Donetz Basin through Upper Silesia, Saxony and the Ruhr Basin to Dusseldorf. Then, one branch will run through Belgium and northern France up Britain to Glasgow, and another branch will go up the Rhine and down the Po, across the Mediterranean and through Egypt to link up with the conurbation round the African Great Lakes. Europe is connected via sea and air lanes with north-east North America, and likewise with the Chinese Peking–Canton conurbation.

'It is,' writes Toynbee, 'a new form of human settlement that has no precedents in mankind's past history. Will human nature be able to stand so radical and so rapid a revolution in mankind's way of life? We do not know the answer. This will be revealed only in the event, and meanwhile, we can do no more than make guesses.'

420 words; Difficulty 7

Further discussion

1 What social problems are associated with the rush to the cities in overpopulated areas?

50 Pollution

'The great question of the 70's is: shall we surrender to our surroundings or shall we make our peace with nature and begin to make reparations for the damage we have done to our air, to our land and to our water?' *President Nixon*

'We have the time – perhaps a generation – in which to save the environment from the final effects of the violence we have done to it.' *Barry Commoner*

'. . . don't drink the water and don't breathe the air!' *Tom Lehrer*

'Mind if I smoke?'

Over the last few years, the public has been made aware of the extent to which man has polluted his planet. The result has been a shock, for no matter how the figures are twisted, the basic prophecy remains: doom with a capital D.

Ecologists are not the most optimistic of people: 'We've already run out of earth, and nothing we can do will keep humankind in existence for as long as another two centuries,' says Martin Litton. But after inspecting all the evidence, nobody laughs at statements like this. Very roughly the problem is as follows: man inhabits the biosphere, the narrow strip of the world between the deepest tree roots and the snowline. This, of course, is connected to the troposphere, which extends upwards to the limit of clouds and weather. Life in these areas is held in a very delicate ecological balance allowing for no waste and no surplus; once the balance is destroyed, as is now happening, all kinds of things start to happen.

Take the example of California, the dream country of thousands. Air pollution has become a serious problem. This is what ecologist, Kenneth Watt, has to say: 'We now have 50% more nitrogen oxides in the air in California ... At the present rate ... it's only a matter of time before light will be filtered out of the atmosphere and none of our land will be usable.' He predicts that air pollution may start a wave of mass deaths by 1985. Already in Los Angeles schools, children are frequently forbidden to take exercise in case they breathe too deeply. So much for air pollution, but that's not all. Physical waste is an enormous problem; the figures are such as to seem meaningless – here are the current ones for the U.S.A. Every year Americans throw away 7 million cars, 100 million tyres, 20 million tons of paper, 28 billion bottles and 48 billion cans. U.S. industry emits 165 million tons of solid waste and 172 million tons of smoke and fumes per annum. This isn't merely a question of banning aluminium cans that won't rot and plastic bottles that can't decay.

Dangerous too are chemical fertilizers and insecticides which upset nature balance at the direct level of ecological food chains. In California where nitrates are used extensively to boost crop production, the land has become unable to fix its own nitrogen and more and more fertilizer has to be used; and the nitrates appear in the water supply where they are a danger to health. The great DDT scandal is now well-known: DDT – a stable substance – was finding its way into food supplies and constituting a great health hazard. The famous French marine biologist, Alain Bombard, believes the sea can dispose of human sewage but that: 'This process of purification is easily and seriously disrupted by the introduction of chemical by-products of civilization.' We have all seen the foam from detergents in rivers, and we all know that rivers go to the sea.

The list of problems is almost endless, but foolproof remedies are hard to find. One example demonstrates this clearly. The United States' water purification plans involve the conversion of organic waste into inorganic compounds which, when introduced into lakes and rivers fertilize aquatic plants which, when they decompose, use the oxygen in the water, and so life in lakes dies. Lake pollution is famous: Leman, Nantua, Erie, etc., etc. The only solution is a widespread change in thinking. Men will have to realize that pollution is a problem with which they themselves as individuals are concerned, but time is the essential factor. The question remains whether it can be done soon enough to preserve the world as a habitable place.

618 words; Difficulty 7

Further discussion

1   What do you consider to be the greatest single source of pollution in your area, and why?

2   Do you think anything further could be done by the authorities to improve the situation?

3   'In my experience as a psychiatrist, noise is the most serious type of pollution. It is also that type which is most easily accepted and therefore the type against which the individual builds up no resistance.' *N. Johnson*. Comment.

4   Why should the individual make an effort to reduce pollution when his small contribution will never even be noticed?

If things go on progressing at their present rate, this may one day be taken as an example of the beauties of nature. After all you can still see the earth, grass and an odd tree . . .

'I do not wish to be hypocritical, but the plain fact is – and we all know it to be true – that whenever we see a story in a newspaper concerning something we know about, it is more often wrong than right.' *John Gordon*

Seeing an inaccuracy in a newspaper report, one's often tempted to condemn that newspaper and its staff out of hand. How can mistakes occur when it is obvious that a paper must have elaborate checking systems to ensure the veracity of its reports?

To investigate the causes of factual mistakes, rather than twists of angle or opinion, a distinction must be made between 'scheduled news' and 'unscheduled news'. With scheduled news – an election, a football match, a trial – a news editor can arrange in advance for one of the paper's reporters to be on the spot; in some cases, the reporter will be aided by special handouts for the press. But unscheduled news – a train or air crash, a suicide, a bank robbery or a riot, for example – is a different matter. How can a harried reporter with a deadline 30 minutes away estimate accurately the number of injured in a train crash that's occurred at midnight in the heart of the country? Can anyone be depended upon to produce a precise assessment of the size of a crowd on the rampage through city streets?

The newsgathering machinery of newspapers is fairly complicated. A large newspaper usually has staff reporters in all the main cities of the country and also part-time correspondents who might be either freelance journalists or on the staff of a provincial paper; they help to extend the net in order to catch the news before it's cold. Other important sources of news are the news agencies which are of great assistance in foreign matters, for a paper can not, for obvious reasons, keep thousands of reporters all over the world just in case a story breaks in front of one of their noses.

Obviously then, mistakes can occur at the source when a paper hasn't got enough reporting strength in the place where a story breaks. Add to this the bewildering variety of stories that a reporter might have to cover, supposedly with expert knowledge of each and every topic, in a single day, and it'll be seen that some errors are inevitable.

A slightly different error is the error of omission, which, although it might come from the source, is often blamed on the sub-editor, who has a great deal to say as to what finally goes into the paper and in what form. To see how mistakes and inaccuracies can occur during the production of the paper, it's necessary to examine the process from beginning to end.

The copy arrives and is considered by the news editor, who may perhaps 'spike' it immediately, or ask for it to be wholly or partly rewritten. Then the 'copy-taster' considers it for appeal to the paper's readership, and decides on the importance that it will be given. Now it's the turn of the sub-editor; he may cut the story and rewrite it completely, or perhaps he will make one story of several versions of the same event. After this, the copy returns to the copy-taster or goes on to the chief sub-editor, where it may be completely revised before reaching the printer. After being set, the piece is read for 'literals' by the proof-readers, goes to the night editor, who checks for inaccuracies and omissions, and is considered by a lawyer for any legal dangers. Frequently, the story will be re-read by the sub-editor, and the reporter if he's available.

Paradoxically, it's in this complex checking machinery that mistakes often occur, for a piece must meet certain requirements: it must be fresh news; it must be the correct length and written in the paper's style; and within the paper it must have an emphasis in line with policy.

In the light of all these factors, one might rather commend the accuracy of the press rather than deplore its mistakes.

640 words; Difficulty 7

Further discussion

1 What moral code can editors have?

2 What sanctions are possible for false information given by the press?

3 Certain information, while true, can do someone harm if published. Has the press the obligation, nevertheless, to publish?

Further practice

The biggest source of further material is the radio. You can record news reports and commentaries, and follow through with the same system.